japan

MARION ELLIOT

japan

GLOBAL DESIGNS FOR NEW LOOK INTERIORS

David & Charles   Trafalgar Square Publishing

For Bill and Sylvia Hadfield

A DAVID & CHARLES BOOK

First published in the UK in 2000
Text copyright © Marion Elliot 2000
Photography and layout copyright © David & Charles 2000
Printed and bound in France by Pollina - n°80869

First published in the UK in 2000 by David & Charles
Brunel House, Newton Abbot, Devon

ISBN 0 7153 1114 X

First published in the United States of America in 2000 by
Trafalgar Square Publishing
North Pomfret, Vermont 05053, USA
ISBN 1-57076-173-6

A catalogue record for this book is available from the British Library.

Commissioning editor   Lindsay Porter
Art editor   Ali Myer
Assistant editor   Jennifer Proverbs
Text editor   Sarah Widdicombe
Designers   Chris and Jane Lanaway
Special photography   Stewart Grant
Styling   Mia Pejcinovic

Contents

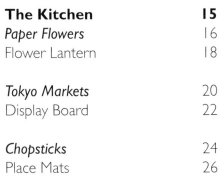

japan
Introduction

For the home designer, Japan is an extremely rich source of inspiration. Look at any photographs of modern or traditional Japan and you will be amazed by the range of colours, materials and textures at your disposal. What could be more inspiring than the calm simplicity of a Bhuddist monk's robes against the raked sand of a temple garden, or the screamingly hot colours of the neon signs that illuminate the night skies of Tokyo? The Japanese gift for combining colours is a lesson in subtlety. Less is definitely more: notice the way that just the right shade of cherry-red is juxtaposed with a cool mint-green, or a flash of

This table top features a Zen garden in miniature.

Subtly coloured handmade paper is used to create books, bound in the traditional Japanese style.

purple iris stands out against the most delicate, lemon-yellow silk kimono.

In recent years, Japanese minimalism has had a huge influence on western interior design. Probably evolving as an antidote to the hectic pace of life, the visual tranquility of pared-down interiors with simple, modular furniture has never seemed so appealing. But pure minimalism is tempered by the desire to cocoon oneself in comfort, hence the trend for luxurious materials

7

such as wool and leather, and richly coloured fabrics. Contrast in textures is also important; poured concrete floors, wenge wood furniture and embroidered throws can co-exist happily in the same room, and artefacts from every part of the world can be combined to create an eclectic, global style.

Light, space and simplicity are the keys to traditional Japanese interior design. House sizes are worked out by calculating how many straw tatami mats can be laid in a grid on the floor, and furniture is kept to a minimum. The rooms are open plan and can be arranged very quickly to fulfil a variety of functions, like eating or sleeping. Intimacy and privacy are created by the use of different types of screens, which divide rooms without taking away the light. The *fusuma*, a large, wooden screen-like structure covered in

" In traditional Japan, the art of interior decorating depends on a heightened sensitivity to the seasons, the personality and interests of the guest of honour and the nature of the social occasion. "

Japanese Style
Slesin, Cliff, Rozensztroch
and De Chabaneix

Garden trellis and plain, transluscent paper create a Japanese-style screen.

paper, is actually a moveable wall, as it runs in grooves in the floor. It can be opened to create one large space, or closed to partition the room into separate areas. Private corners can be created with the *byobu* screen, a series of hinged panels covered with paper. To make an authentic-looking Japanese screen, simply glue lengths of tracing paper to the back of three garden trellises and hinge them together.

Extend the idea to the bedroom to introduce a subtle Japanese theme with a trellis

Richly coloured, luxurious satins combine to make a striking quilt.

light screen (see page 36). This provides a stylish cover-up for a wall light and, at the same time, diffuses the light beautifully, casting a hazy glow throughout the room. Re-arrange your furniture to give the room an authentic, symmetrical appearance and be ruthless with clutter, packing away what you don't need. Subtlety works well here: the wonderful, rich colours of the quilted blanket on pages 28-9 make such a strong impact, that nothing else is needed.

Traditionally, Japanese life is conducted at floor level. Food is eaten while seated on the floor, and a simple futon mattress provides a bed. While wall-to-wall Japanese style would be too much for

Wall lights are concealed behind small screens in the bedroom.

many western homes (unless you happen to live in

a loft, or inhabit a modernist masterpiece!),

certain elements can be incorporated to great

effect. Low-level furniture works beautifully with

the current trend for casual living, where the only

seating may be a leather foot-stool or a couple of

cushions. If you live in a studio, where eating,

sleeping and living all take place in one room, live

like the Japanese and divide off areas with

moveable screens: the paper panels will provide

cover without taking away the natural light.

Bathing is an important ritual in Japan and

involves more than just personal cleanliness – it

also has overtones of purification that linger from

the ancient Shinto religion. Historically,

communal bath houses were an important place

in the local communities, where friends could

meet and exchange gossip. Although many homes

" ...I saw numerous

pavilions with brocade

curtains, closed off

by bright green blinds

and surrounded

by hangings. "

The Pillow Book of
Sei Shonagon

now have private tubs,

bath houses are still in

use today, as are the

naturally occurring

hot-spring pools found

throughout Japan. The

This pebble panel echoes the ordered design of traditional rock gardens.

primary function of the bath is to provide bathers

with a long, relaxing soak in very hot water. As

some communal baths may be large enough to

hold many people, it is essential that the water

remains clean and pleasant. To ensure this, the

bathers wash themselves first, rinsing away all

traces of soap before entering the bath.

As the bathroom is one of the most

important rooms in the house, and a place to soak

away the worries of the day, why not inject a little

of the order and sensual pleasure of the Japanese

bath house? Traditionally, tubs are made from

soft cedar wood, which gives off a subtle aroma when immersed in water. Burn delicately perfumed incense around the bath or scent your bathwater to replicate the same delicious smell. Extend the organic theme with a polished pebble panel (see page 46), and imitate the Japanese love of bamboo with a duckboard mat (see page 50) in place of a traditional western bathmat.

As you will see, inspiration is to be found in every aspect of Japanese style, and all the designs in this book can be adapted to suit your own individual needs. The idea is not to replicate a Japanese home but simply to borrow the most appropriate and inspiring elements and fashion them to your own surroundings. So, empty your mind – and your home – of clutter, think Japanese, and create a personal space infused with Zen tranquility.

A bathroom duckboard mat is created from lengths of bamboo bound with string.

japan
The Kitchen

" *One after another the guests*

took the bowl and, after holding it

for a while, poured some of the

wine into a thing called a Yaku

shell and drank. "

The Pillow Book of Sei Shonagon

15

Paper Flowers

In Japan, paper crafts are held in high esteem. The best known form is origami, where paper is folded in a particular sequence to make small models. Paper flowers made from brightly coloured tissue paper are used as decoration in a variety of children's festivals. Paper crafts in general are celebrated during the summer at the Star Festival, when immensely complex tissue-paper creations are displayed.

For the flower lantern, brightly coloured handmade Japanese papers are collaged onto a traditional paper lantern. Paper flowers are arranged in three bands, divided by thin paper strips, while the top of the lantern is encircled by a ring of tissue-paper flowers. The paper tassel at the base adds an oriental touch. The lantern has a stained-glass quality when lit at night.

Flower Lantern

Materials & Equipment

- Paper lantern
- Handmade paper in orange, lime-green, pink, blue and red
- Pencil and ruler
- Scissors
- Wallpaper paste and brush
- Pair of compasses (compass)
- Pinking shears
- Tissue paper in assorted bright colours, including orange and pink
- Stapler
- Craft knife
- Masking tape
- Needle and red cotton embroidery thread

1 Assemble the lantern. Cut a band 10cm (4in) wide from orange handmade paper and glue it around the middle of the lantern using wallpaper paste.

SAFETY NOTE: Do not use a light bulb greater than 40W power in this lantern.

2 Using a pair of compasses (compass), draw circles 8cm (3in) in diameter onto orange, lime-green, pink and blue paper and cut them out. Using wallpaper paste, glue them around the orange band, and above and below it.

3 To make the flowers, draw and cut out more circles 8cm (3in) in diameter from the paper colours used so far, plus red. Fold each circle into eighths.

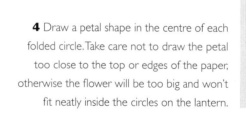

4 Draw a petal shape in the centre of each folded circle. Take care not to draw the petal too close to the top or edges of the paper, otherwise the flower will be too big and won't fit neatly inside the circles on the lantern.

5 Grip the paper firmly to keep all the layers together and cut carefully around the petal. Unfold the circle to reveal the flower.

6 Glue the flowers to contrasting circles around the lantern using wallpaper paste. Cut out small circles from the various paper colours and glue one in the centre of each flower.

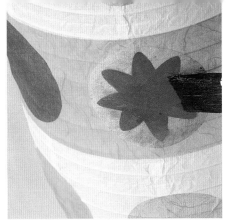

8 Cut strips 10cm (4in) wide from tissue paper in assorted bright colours and fold each one over lengthwise to make a double strip 5cm (2in) wide. Fold in half widthwise. Clip along the unfolded edge of each strip, almost as far as the long fold, to make a fringe.

7 Using pinking shears, cut two strips 1.5cm (½in) wide from red paper to fit around the circumference of the lantern. Using wallpaper paste, glue one strip to the top of the lantern, just below the opening. Glue a second strip above the orange band in the middle of the lantern.

9 Roll the unclipped edge of the paper around a pencil to make a flower shape. Staple the ends of the flower to keep them together. Fluff out the petals to make a pompom shape.

10 Using a craft knife, cut small, equally spaced slits around the top of the lantern to hold the pompom flowers. Push the end of a flower through each slit and secure it in place with masking tape on the inside of the lantern.

11 Cut a strip 40cm (16in) wide from orange tissue paper and a similar strip from pink. Following steps 8 and 9, clip and roll the papers together to make a long tassel. Thread the tassel onto a length of red cotton embroidery thread. To suspend the tassel from the lantern, tie the thread to the metal strut at the base and trim off the ends.

19

Tokyo Markets

Tokyo shops are famous for their piles of multi-coloured produce, stacked in neat rows and crowded into densely packed wall displays. The bustling Tsukiji market, the largest fish market in the world, sells an enormous array of wares, ranging from fish and seafood to vegetables and cooking pots, which are found in the street markets outside.

The kitchen display board echoes the exuberance of Tokyo shops, with its lively colours and hanging display. Thick peg board is mounted on wooden blocks and painted a vivid lime-green. A flash of shocking-pink paint is added along the top edge. Peg-board hangers are inserted into the holes and vividly coloured packets of Japanese foodstuffs, with arresting graphic designs, are hung from the hooks.

Display Board

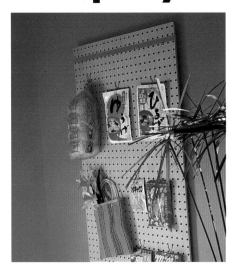

Materials & Equipment

- Sheet of 6mm (¼in) perforated hardboard, 120 x 60cm (48 x 24in)
- 4 blocks of 15mm (½in) MDF (medium-density fibreboard), each 7 x 7cm (2¾ x 2¾in)
- Waterproof wood adhesive
- 25mm (1in) panel pins (tacks) and hammer
- Clamp • Scrap wood
- Hand drill
- Water-based acrylic wood primer
- Small emulsion (latex) paint roller
- Lime-green emulsion (latex) paint
- Low-tack masking tape
- Raspberry-red acrylic paint
- Old saucer • Paintbrush
- Spirit (carpenter's) level • Pencil
- Rawl plugs (wall anchors)
- 4 dome-head screws
- Screwdriver
- Metal peg-board hangers or 6mm (¼in) wooden dowel pegs

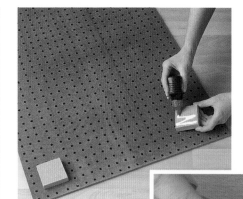

1 Place the sheet of perforated hardboard face down. Glue one MDF block in each corner of the board, 2cm (¾in) in from each edge, using waterproof wood adhesive. Remove any excess adhesive from the front of the hardboard with a damp cloth.

2 When the adhesive is dry, turn the board over and tap panel pins (tacks) through the board into the blocks below to strengthen the join.

3 Clamp the board firmly to scrap wood. Using an existing hole towards the centre of the block as your starting point, drill through each block once from the front of the board, so that it can be screwed to the wall.

22

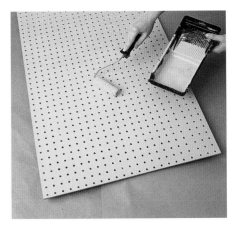

4 Apply one coat of acrylic wood primer to the front of the board, using a small roller to avoid clogging the holes. When the primer is dry, apply two coats of lime-green emulsion (latex) paint.

5 Using low-tack masking tape, mask off a narrow area at the top of the board. The first strip of tape should be positioned one hole down from the top edge of the board.

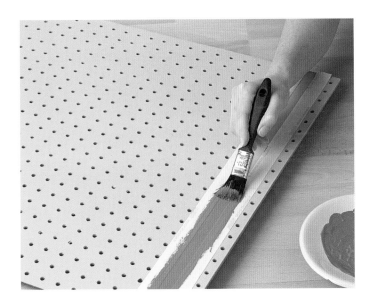

6 Mix raspberry-red acrylic paint with a little water in an old saucer. Brush the paint over the masked-off area at the top of the board to create a thin stripe. When the paint is dry, carefully peel away the masking tape.

7 Place the board against the wall and use a spirit (carpenter's) level to check that it is straight. Mark the position of the drilled holes on the wall. Remove the board and drill the wall where marked, then insert rawl plugs (wall anchors). Screw the board to the wall using dome-head screws.

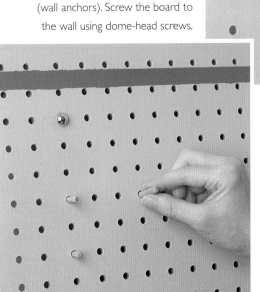

8 Insert metal peg-board hangers and/or window dowel pegs into the holes and hang up kitchen utensils and food packets.

Chopsticks

In Japan, food is traditionally served in small pieces that can be picked up one by one with chopsticks. Everyday chopsticks are made of wood, and are often disposable. For more formal occasions, beautifully decorated chopsticks made from lacquered wood or china are used. Chopsticks are never left in the food between each mouthful, as this is considered unlucky. Instead they are placed on small rests beside the bowl to keep them clean.

These place mats are made from pairs of disposable wooden chopsticks. These are tinted a deep colour with waterproof artist's ink, then a notch is sawn into the wood at top and bottom. The chopsticks are placed in a row in alternate directions, then tied together with strong cotton thread to make a solid mat.

Place Mats

Materials & Equipment

- 20 pairs of joined wooden chopsticks
- Waterproof artist's ink
- Paintbrush
- Pencil and ruler
- Cutting mat
- Hacksaw
- Scissors
- Cotton embroidery thread
- Silk tassel

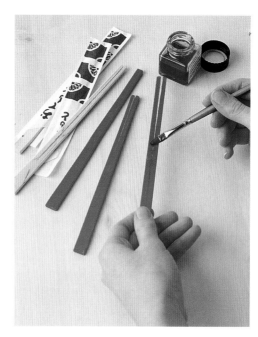

1 Paint the chopsticks with artist's ink and leave to dry. You may have to apply a second coat to achieve a deep colour.

2 Using a pencil and ruler, mark a point 3cm (1¼in) along from the top and bottom of each pair of chopsticks.

3 Place the chopsticks on a cutting mat. Using a hacksaw, make a shallow cut across the top and bottom of the chopsticks where marked to create notches.

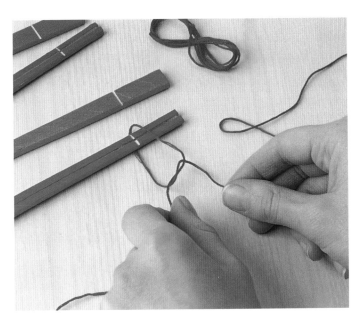

4 Cut two lengths of cotton embroidery thread each 60cm (24in) long and double them over. Place a pair of chopsticks in the looped ends of the thread, with a loop resting in each notch. Tie the thread firmly around the notches.

It has often been said that the Japanese eat with their eyes. Food is always presented in artistic compositions of shape and colour.

Culture Shock! Japan
Rex Shelley

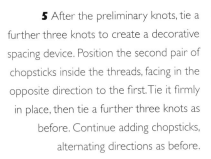

5 After the preliminary knots, tie a further three knots to create a decorative spacing device. Position the second pair of chopsticks inside the threads, facing in the opposite direction to the first. Tie it firmly in place, then tie a further three knots as before. Continue adding chopsticks, alternating directions as before.

6 When you have used all 20 pairs of chopsticks, tie off the ends of the thread tightly. Trim the upper threads to 1cm (⅜in) long and leave the lower threads longer.

7 Loop a silk tassel onto the lower threads and tie tightly. Trim the ends of the threads.

japan
The Bedroom

> " *When I awoke late at*
>
> *night, the moonlight was pouring*
>
> *in through the window and*
>
> *shining on the bed-clothes of all*
>
> *the other people in the room.*
>
> *Its clear white brilliance moved*
>
> *me greatly...* "

The Pillow Book of Sei Shonagon

The Kimono

The kimono is worn by both men and women in Japan. A deceptively simple garment, it may be of plain cotton or intricately decorated, woven silk. The kimono is traditionally made from seven pieces of fabric and is held together with a wide sash called an *obi*. As with all traditional Japanese design, a great deal of thought is given to the colours and motifs used in kimonos, resulting in some spectacularly beautiful designs.

This reversible quilt draws its inspiration from these stunning colour combinations and is made from squares of heavyweight shot-satin in chartreuse-green, purple and claret. The fabric was chosen for its wonderful light-reflecting qualities; the colours appear to change and shimmer when they catch the light.

Patchwork Quilt

Materials & Equipment

- Thick card (cardboard)
- Pencil and ruler
- Scissors
- Tailor's chalk
- 1.5m (1¾yd) chartreuse-green shot satin, 150cm (60in) wide
- 0.75m (¾yd) each claret and purple shot satin, 150cm (60in) wide
- Dressmaker's pins
- Tacking (basting) thread and needle
- Piece of 125g (4oz) wadding (batting) to fit quilt
- 2m (2¼yd) shot brocade, 140cm (56in) wide
- Sewing needle
- Sewing machine and threads to match fabrics

1 Draw a 25cm (10in) square onto thick card (cardboard) and cut it out. Draw around the template onto your fabrics using tailor's chalk. To make a quilt measuring 178 × 132cm (70 × 52in), you will need 24 green squares, 12 claret and 12 purple. Cut out all the squares.

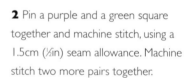

2 Pin a purple and a green square together and machine stitch, using a 1.5cm (½in) seam allowance. Machine stitch two more pairs together.

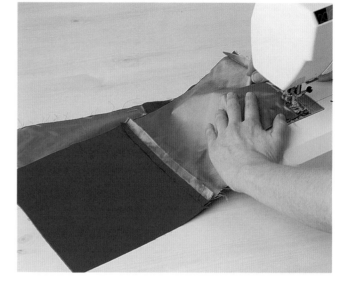

3 Pin the three pairs of squares together, beginning with a green square and alternating colours, to make a row six squares long. Machine stitch as before. Join the remaining green and purple squares, beginning with a purple square to make three more rows of six squares each. Repeat to join the green and claret squares, beginning with a green square.

4 Press open all the seams. Pin and tack (baste) a row of purple and green squares above a row of claret and green, matching the seamlines and edges exactly. Repeat, alternating colours, to make a patchwork six squares wide and eight squares deep. Machine stitch the rows together, remove the tacking stitches and then press open the seams.

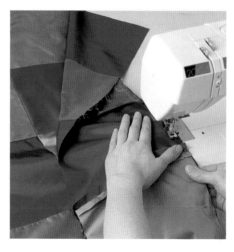

5 Place the patchwork face down. Cut a piece of wadding (batting) to the same size and pin it to the back of the fabric. Tack firmly in position, matching the corners and edges exactly.

6 For the backing, cut a piece of brocade to the same size as the patchwork. Pin and tack (baste) the backing to the quilt, right sides together. Machine stitch the layers together, using a 1.5cm (⅝in) seam allowance. Leave a 30cm (12in) opening along one edge.

7 Clip the corners of the quilt and trim the side seams. Turn through the quilt and press lightly using a cool iron. Turn in the raw edges of the opening, then slipstitch the edges together using thread to match the quilt backing.

8 Shake the quilt so that all the layers of fabric lie flat. To keep the quilt straight, sew a tailor's tack at the corner of each square, through all the layers of fabric.

9 Overstitch the seamlines on the front of the patchwork, through all the layers, to quilt the fabric. Stitch only on the green fabric, using matching thread, and match the bobbin thread to the quilt backing. Remove all the tailor's tacks.

33

Fusuma Screens

When panelled wooden screens were introduced to Japan from China, they immediately became an integral part of the traditional Japanese home. The Japanese refined the screens to suit their way of life, constructing lightweight, trellis-style wooden panels covered with sheets of handmade paper. The paper diffused daylight, creating a soft, hazy effect. Known as *fusuma*, these screens were designed to partition rooms and could be opened and closed, as they ran along grooves in the floor.

The wall light in this bedroom scheme is based on traditional *fusuma* screens. A length of garden trellis is cut to size and mounted on wooden battens, with handmade paper attached to the back. The screen is then positioned over a low-wattage light which casts a soft glow.

Wall Light

Materials & Equipment

- Nine-square section of wooden garden trellis
- Waterproof wood adhesive
- 2 strips of 15mm (½in) birch-faced ply, each 8cm (3in) wide x length of trellis
- 15mm (½in) panel pins (tacks) and hammer
- Protective face mask
- Fine-grade sandpaper
- Water-based dark oak wood stain
- Paintbrush • Lint-free cloth
- Pencil • Metal safety ruler
- Sheet of thin white Japanese paper, height of trellis x width plus 5cm (2in)
- Craft knife and cutting mat
- Fire retardant • PVA adhesive (all-purpose white glue)
- Two 7cm (2¾in) L-shaped metal brackets and screws
- Screwdriver
- 40W self-adhesive battery-operated light
- Hand drill

1 Referring to the diagram at the back of the book, place the trellis face down. Spread waterproof wood adhesive along the side of one of the batten strips and glue it to the back of the trellis along one side, lining up the sides exactly. Repeat to attach the second batten to the other side of the trellis. Wipe off any excess adhesive with a damp cloth.

2 When the adhesive is dry, turn the frame over. Tap panel pins (tacks) down the sides of the trellis to strengthen the join between trellis and battens.

3 Wearing a face mask, lightly sand the frame, then apply a coat of dark oak wood stain, following the grain of the wood.

4 Before the wood stain dries completely, remove the excess from the frame using a soft, lint-free cloth. Leave to dry.

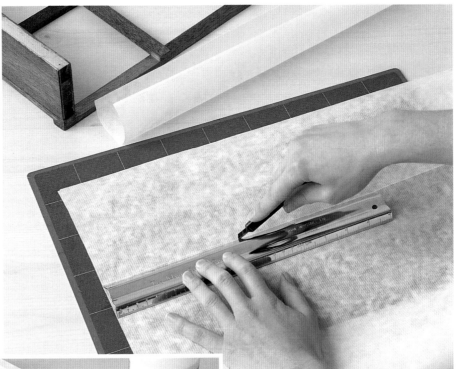

5 Measure the gaps between the struts of wood and cut three strips of thin white Japanese paper to the same length and slightly wider. The extra width will be folded upwards so that it rests against the sides of the struts when the paper is in position. Apply a coat of fire retardant to the paper and leave to dry.

6 Spread PVA adhesive (white glue) onto the horizontal struts at the back of the trellis. Press the paper into position and trim if necessary. Leave to dry.

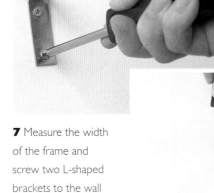

7 Measure the width of the frame and screw two L-shaped brackets to the wall to support it at either side. Attach a self-adhesive light to the wall in the centre of the area.

8 Place the frame in position, resting against the brackets. Mark the positions of the holes on the frame and drill a pilot hole at each mark. Screw the frame firmly to the brackets.

Silk Handbags

Delicate, embroidery-covered silk handbags are as popular an accessory in Japan as in the West. They are the perfect accompaniment to a beautiful silk kimono. This handbag is adorned with a portrait of a geisha, the traditional female entertainer skilled in the arts of singing, classical dance and conversation. Traditional geisha apparel includes sumptuous kimonos, tall wooden shoes and ornately dressed hair. Even their trademark white complexions are exotic, enhanced by powder and applications of nightingale droppings!

The geisha bag is made from delicately sprigged, finely woven cotton. The image of the geisha is applied to the green cotton fabric using transfer paste, and then edged with satin ribbon. Small buttons are sewn at the base of the handles.

Geisha Bag

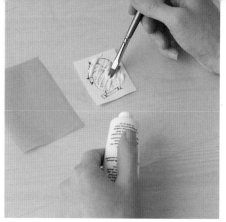

1 Photocopy the picture of the geisha girl from the back of the book, reducing it to your desired size, and cut it out. Cut a piece of cotton fabric slightly larger than the photocopy. Following the manufacturer's instructions, paint transfer paste over the picture and press it face down onto the fabric to transfer the image.

Materials & Equipment

- Scissors
- Plain cotton fabric, for picture
- Image transfer paste
- Paintbrush
- Sponge
- 0.5m (¾yd) patterned cotton fabric, 90cm (36in) wide, for bag
- 0.3m (½yd) patterned cotton fabric, 90cm (36in) wide, for lining
- Dressmaker's pins
- Length of ruffled satin ribbon to fit around picture
- Tacking (basting) thread and needle
- Sewing needle
- 2 buttons
- Sewing machine and threads to match fabrics

2 Dampen the back of the picture with a sponge and peel off the excess paper from the fabric. Leave the picture to dry.

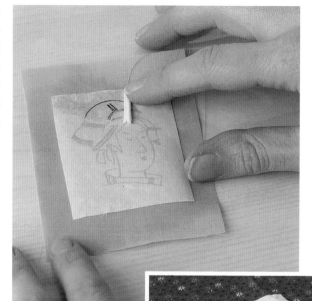

3 Enlarge the bag patterns from the back of the book on a photocopier. Cut out the pattern pieces: cut one front, one back, two gussets, one base and two handles from the bag fabric, and the same, except for the handles, from the lining fabric.

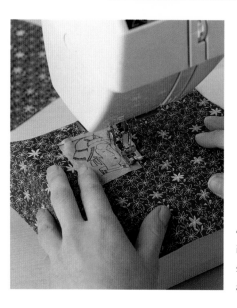

4 Neatly trim the geisha picture and pin it to the centre of the bag front. Machine stitch the picture in place, using as narrow a seam allowance as possible.

5 With right sides together, pin the base to the bag front (if you are using reversible fabric, the gussets and base make a contrast). Machine stitch using a 1.5cm (½in) seam allowance, to within 1.5cm (½in) of either end. With right sides facing, pin the gussets to the bag front. Machine stitch the gussets in place, to within 1.5cm (½in) of the bottom of the bag.

6 Pin the ends of the gussets to the sides of the bag base. Machine stitch in place, to within 1.5cm (½in) of the end of the far side. Machine stitch a length of ruffled ribbon around the geisha picture to make a border.

7 Pin the bag back to the gussets and base, and machine stitch in place. Repeat steps 5–7 to assemble the bag lining.

8 Clip the corners of the bag and press open the seams. Turn through. Insert the lining, wrong side out, into the bag. Pin and tack (baste) the top edge of the lining and the bag together. Machine stitch. Turn over the top of the bag by 1.5cm (½in). Press under the raw edge and slipstitch the turning.

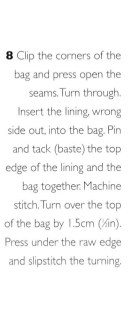

9 Press the handles in half, right sides together. Machine stitch along the side and one end, using a 1cm (⅜in) seam allowance. Clip the corners and trim the seams, then turn through the handles and press. Turn in the raw edges at the end of each handle and slipstitch the opening.

10 Pin the handles to the front and back of the bag, 2cm (¾in) in from the side seams. Machine stitch the handles in place. On the front of the bag, sew a button centrally at the base of each handle as decoration.

japan
The
Bathroom

" *A soak in such a tub is*

an indescribable pleasure,

enhanced by the softness of the

wood and by the gentle aroma it

gives off when wet. "

All Japan:
The Catalogue of Everything Japanese
Oliver Statler

Garden Paths

Large, flat, black rocks are a common feature in Japanese gardens and are used to make paths and create walkways. Sometimes they are used in combination with water, for example to line the bottom of hot-spring pools. The rocks are arranged randomly in an all-over design, and set into light-coloured cement so that they resemble free-form mosaic. In gardens, they make a strong visual impact among finely raked sand and moss-covered rocks.

This pebble panel is an eye-catching and organic element of the bathroom, integral to the natural theme of the room. Small, flat pebbles are set into white cement to make a bold, graphic design. They are placed in vertical rows, rather than randomly, to echo the sense of order in the rest of the bathroom.

Pebble Panel

Materials & Equipment

- 15mm- ($\frac{1}{2}$in-) thick marine plywood, to fit area above bath
- Wood sealant
- Paintbrush • Marine varnish
- Craft knife
- Waterproof wood adhesive
- Strips of 25mm- (1in-) wide wooden batten, to fit around plywood
- 15mm ($\frac{1}{2}$in) panel pins (tacks) and hammer
- Filler and filler knife
- Smooth black pebbles
- Pencil and ruler
- Clamp • Scrap wood
- Hand drill
- Masking tape
- Blackboard paint and 15mm ($\frac{1}{2}$in) paintbrush
- 50mm (2in) screws
- Protective face mask
- Cement-based waterproof tile adhesive
- Rubber-edged spreader
- Waterproof grout
- 25mm (1in) paintbrush
- Rawl plugs (wall anchors)

1 Apply a coat of wood sealant to the front and back of the plywood and leave to dry. Waterproof the back of the board with two coats of marine varnish.

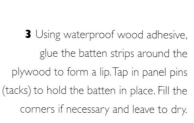

2 Using a craft knife, score the front of the plywood in a cross-hatched pattern. This creates a surface for the tile adhesive to bond to.

3 Using waterproof wood adhesive, glue the batten strips around the plywood to form a lip. Tap in panel pins (tacks) to hold the batten in place. Fill the corners if necessary and leave to dry.

5 Mask off the inside edges of the panel, then apply two coats of blackboard paint to the battens. When the paint is dry, remove the masking tape. Insert screws loosely into the drilled holes to keep them open.

4 Place a row of pebbles at either side of the plywood to determine the position of the screw holes that will attach the panel to the wall. Mark the holes. Clamp the panel to scrap wood and drill a hole at each mark.

6 Wearing a face mask, mix the tile adhesive following the manufacturer's instructions. Spread a smooth layer of adhesive 2mm (1/16in) thick over a 15cm- (6in-) square area of the panel, using a rubber-edged spreader.

7 Press the pebbles into the adhesive, flat side down. Continue to lay adhesive and pebbles over a small area at a time, until the panel is covered. Leave to dry thoroughly. Using a 25mm (1in) paintbrush, spread a thin layer of grout around the pebbles. Wipe away any excess with a damp cloth before it dries. Leave the panel to dry for several days, then attach to the wall with rawl plugs (wall anchors) and screws.

Bamboo Fences

In addition to Zen gardens, two main types of Japanese garden are the tea garden and the pond garden. Tea gardens provide a serene and understated approach to a tea house. They may be very small, especially in urban areas, but are always beautifully designed and never look cluttered. Pond gardens are beautiful, contemplative spaces, containing bridges, landscaping and magnificent trees. The gardens are often bounded by rustic fences, made from lengths of thick bamboo.

The duckboard gives a rustic feel to the bathroom, while the smooth bamboo canes feel warm to the touch and massage the soles of the feet. Medium-width canes are lashed tightly across supporting canes in a decorative, stylized way, in imitation of a Japanese garden fence.

Bamboo Duckboard

Materials & Equipment

- 10.5m (13ft) bamboo, 3cm (1¼in) in diameter
- Clamp
- Hacksaw
- Protective face mask
- Medium- and fine-grade sandpaper and sanding block
- String and scissors
- Dark brown cotton gimp
- Matt acrylic varnish and paintbrush

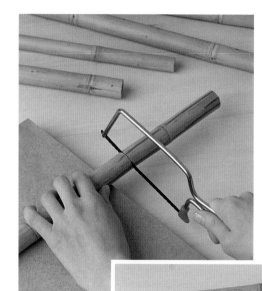

1 Clamp and cut three 50cm (20in) lengths and fourteen 65cm (26in) lengths of bamboo.

2 Wearing a face mask, sand the canes all over, especially the cut ends, to remove any rough patches or splinters.

3 Place the three shorter canes on a flat surface. Lay two longer pieces of bamboo horizontally over them, one at the top and one at the bottom. Tie the canes temporarily with string to make the duckboard frame.

5 Pull the cotton gimp over to the other side of the joint and wrap it around another 15 times, this time from upper left to lower right.

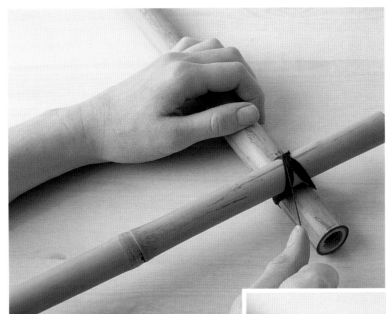

4 Turn the duckboard over. Working on the central cane first, and then those at each end, remove the string and securely tie on a length of brown cotton gimp to attach the upper cane firmly to the cane below. Wrap the cotton gimp diagonally 15 times around the joint, from upper right to lower left.

6 Tie the end of the cotton gimp tightly around the joint in a loop. Pass the end to the back of the duckboard and tie it off very tightly. Trim the ends.

7 Tie on two more canes in the same way, one at either side of the central strut. Working from the centre outwards, continue to attach canes to either side of the duckboard until it is complete. Leave a small gap between each pair of canes as you work to allow water to drain through. Seal the duckboard with two coats of matt varnish and leave to dry thoroughly. Place the duckboard on a non-slip surface before use.

Floating Lanterns

During August, the *Bon*, or All-Souls' Festival, is celebrated to welcome the souls of ancestors back to the world. Offerings of food are made to the departed at family altars, and incense and lanterns are lit at family graves. At the end of the festival, lighted paper lanterns are floated on water to mark the departure of the ancestors' spirits once more.

This tea-light block is cast from fine plaster, inside a rectangular wooden mould. The clean, minimalist lines of the block and the smoothness of the plaster surface give it a calm and soothing ambience. Before the plaster sets, a row of five tea lights in metal containers are pushed slowly into the block to make permanent recesses. More or fewer tea lights can be used as desired, to achieve different levels of light.

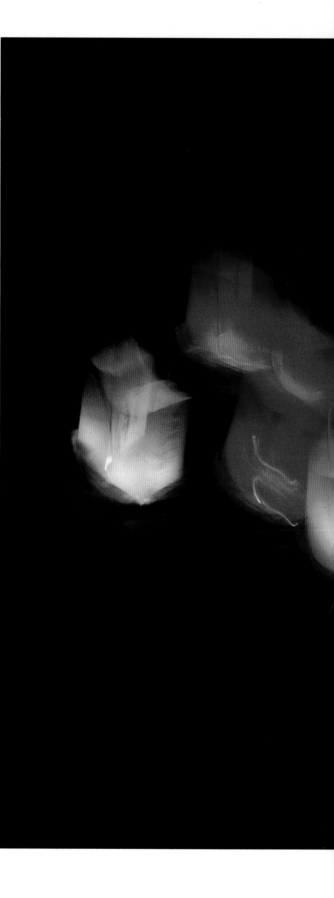

Plaster Candleholder

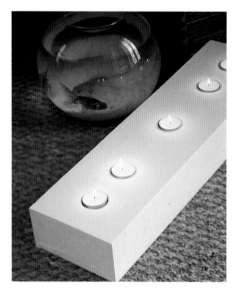

Materials & Equipment

- Clamp
- 2 pieces of 18mm (⅝in) MDF (medium-density fibreboard) each 60 x 12cm (24 x 4½in), for side walls
- Drill with countersink bit
- 2 pieces of 18mm (⅝in) MDF, each 16 x 12cm (6¼ x 4½in), for ends
- Screwdriver and screws
- 1 piece of 18mm (⅝in) MDF, 65 x 30cm (26 x 12in), for base
- Pencil and ruler
- Modelling clay • Plastic sheet
- Plastic bucket
- Fine casting plaster and plastic scoop
- Rubber gloves • Protective face mask
- Wooden stick • Mesh sieve
- 5 tea lights in metal holders
- Pliers • Fine-grade sandpaper

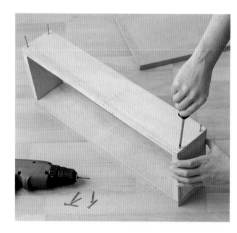

1 Referring to the diagram at the back of the book, clamp the side walls of the candleholder mould to your work surface. At each corner, measure and drill a point 2cm (¾in) down from the long edge. Mark corresponding holes in the edges of the end walls, then clamp them and drill a pilot hole at each point. Screw the walls together to make a rectangular box.

2 Before screwing the box to the base of the mould, position it centrally and mark the outer and inner edges of each wall. Measure a point 1cm (⅜in) down and in from each corner, then clamp the base and drill a hole at each point.

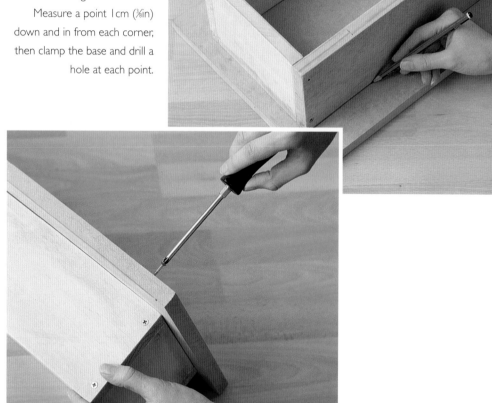

3 Mark and drill matching pilot holes in the base of the box. Screw the box tightly to the base to complete the mould.

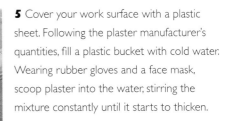

5 Cover your work surface with a plastic sheet. Following the plaster manufacturer's quantities, fill a plastic bucket with cold water. Wearing rubber gloves and a face mask, scoop plaster into the water, stirring the mixture constantly until it starts to thicken.

4 To make the mould watertight, press small pellets of clay around the lower edge of the box, sealing the join.

6 Rest a mesh sieve on the mould. Position the bucket over the sieve and pour the plaster slowly into the mould. Try not to splash as you pour, otherwise you will get lots of air bubbles in the plaster. Keep some clay to hand so that you can plug any breaks in the seal immediately.

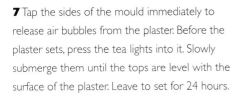

7 Tap the sides of the mould immediately to release air bubbles from the plaster. Before the plaster sets, press the tea lights into it. Slowly submerge them until the tops are level with the surface of the plaster. Leave to set for 24 hours.

8 Positioning one corner of the mould at a time over the edge of your work surface, unscrew the base from underneath. Unscrew the walls from each other. Leave the plaster block to dry thoroughly for two weeks, then remove the tea lights and metal holders using pliers. Wearing a face mask, lightly sand the plaster smooth. Sand around the edges of the holes to enlarge them slightly so that the tea-light holders can be removed easily.

japan

The Study

" *...for it was not until AD 770 that*

the first text printing upon paper was finally

completed...this original printing of

Empress Shotuku's 'dharani' took place

in Japan... "

Papermaking:
The History and Technique of an Ancient Craft
Dard Hunter

Flower Symbols

Japan is particularly rich in symbolic flower images. For example, the chrysanthemum has been the traditional crest of the Imperial family since the twelfth century – it represents longevity and happiness. Other interesting symbolic flowers include peach blossom, which denotes spring and marriage; the peony, which indicates marriage and fertility; and cherry blossom, which denotes prosperity and riches.

The stencilled border is a simple, repeated flower motif that runs along the wall at dado (chair rail) height. The design is cut into stencil card (cardboard) and stencilled onto a narrow paper band. Acrylic paint is used for the stencil, as it becomes waterproof once dry and won't run when wallpaper paste is applied. The lining paper was left plain, but it could be painted first.

Flower Border

Materials & Equipment

- Pencil and metal safety ruler
- Oiled manilla stencil card (cardboard)
- Tracing paper
- Scissors
- Craft knife and cutting mat
- Lining paper
- Paintbrush
- Red acrylic paint
- Old saucer
- Natural sponge
- Scrap paper
- Eraser
- Wallpaper paste and brush

1 Draw a 6cm (2½in) square on a piece of stencil card (cardboard). Trace the flower pattern from the back of the book and transfer it to the stencil card, placing it centrally inside the square.

2 Cut out the square using scissors and place it on a cutting mat. Using a craft knife, cut out the petals and centre of the flower to make a stencil.

3 Decide on the length of your border. Cut a band of lining paper 6cm (2½in) wide and to the required length. If you prefer, for ease of handling, you can cut two or three shorter strips to make up the full length.

5 Using a paintbrush, mix red acrylic paint with a little water in an old saucer. The paint should be sticky, but not too thick. Place the stencil at the start of the border.

4 Place the stencil at the beginning of the border strip, aligned with the upper and lower edges. Mark the position of the right-hand side of the stencil with a faint pencil line. Move the stencil along the border, marking the right-hand side each time, to make a spacing guide.

6 Pick up a little of the paint on the end of a natural sponge and press it onto the paper through the stencil. Dab paint around the flower until the whole design is stencilled.

8 Replace the stencil on the border, lining up the left-hand side against the next pencil line. Continue stencilling to complete the border. Erase the pencil lines if they show. Glue the border to the wall using wallpaper paste.

7 Lift the stencil straight up from the border, to avoid smudging the paint. Place the stencil on scrap paper and blot the front and back, to remove excess paint.

Women's Dress

The subtle pairing of contrasting colours, as seen in the soft green and striking red garments of these women, is typical of the sophistication of traditional and ceremonial dress in Japan. There are various styles of traditional women's dress. The kimono is the best known, worn usually on formal occasions. There are also flowing gowns, similar to kimonos, that are worn over plain, sleeveless shifts.

These hand-stitched books echo the soft colours of the women's dresses. After papermaking spread from China to Japan in about the seventh century, the Japanese swiftly became master papermakers, creating exceptionally strong, high-quality paper. Both books contain pages of handmade Japanese paper, sewn together in the traditional way.

Hand-bound Books

Materials & Equipment

- A3 (16½ x 12in) sheet of thin white card (cardboard)
- Safety ruler and pencil
- Craft knife and cutting mat
- Paper adhesive
- A3 (16½ x 12in) sheet of green handmade paper
- Scissors
- Three A2 (24 x16½in) sheets of white handmade paper
- Three A2 (24 x16½in) sheets of tracing paper
- Bradawl (awl)
- 2 buttons
- Darning needle
- Red cotton embroidery thread
- Flowered paper
- Thick red embroidery silk

1 For the front and back cover, cut two pieces of thin card (cardboard) measuring 30 × 13cm (12 × 5in). Draw a 5cm (2in) square on the right-hand side of one piece of card about 3cm (1¼in) from the right-hand edge and cut it out to make an opening.

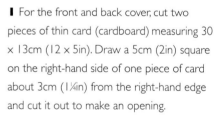

2 Glue both pieces of card (cardboard) to the green handmade paper. Trim down the paper using a craft knife and ruler, leaving a 2cm (¾in) border.

3 Snip the corners of the handmade paper diagonally, just above the card (cardboard). Fold the borders over the edges of the book covers and glue them in place.

4 Place the front cover face down on a cutting mat. Cut diagonally in both directions across the paper where it covers the opening. Fold the paper to the inside of the cover and glue in place. Cut a rectangle of white handmade paper slightly smaller than the cover, with a matching opening. Glue to the back of the front cover. Repeat for the back cover.

5 Cut 10 pieces of white paper and 10 pieces of tracing paper, each measuring 58 × 12.5cm (23 × 4¾in). Fold them all in half to make the pages and picture protectors.

6 Lightly score the back of the front cover with a craft knife, about 4cm (1½in) in from the side. Fold the cover upwards to crease it slightly. Repeat for the back cover.

7 Referring to the diagram at the back of the book, use a bradawl (awl) to pierce holes every 1.5cm (½in) down the left-hand side of the front and back covers and pages.

8 Position a button centrally on the right-hand side of the front cover. Pierce through the buttonholes into the card (cardboard) using a bradawl (awl). Place the front cover on top of the back and pierce matching holes.

9 Assemble the book, interleaving plain and tracing paper and lining up all the holes. Thread a darning needle with a length of red cotton embroidery thread. Starting at the lower edge of the spine, sew the book together using blanket stitch.

10 Sew the buttons in place on the front and the back covers using red cotton embroidery thread. Tie off the ends neatly on the inside of each cover.

11 Cut a piece of flowered paper slightly larger than the opening in the front cover and glue it directly underneath, onto the first page. Cut a length of thick red embroidery silk. Loop it around the bottom button and then wind it around the buttons from the front to the back of the book, to keep it fastened.

65

Japanese shoes

The most common type of traditional Japanese shoe is a kind of heeled flip-flop, called *zori*. Wooden shoes called *geta* are also widely worn. Geta shoes fit flat against the foot and are raised several inches high on two wooden supports. Solid wooden shoes that taper away below the toes are also worn. Traditional Japanese shoes have two central thongs that fit between the first two toes.

The tea-house tray is inspired by traditional wooden shoes. It is supported on four short, round legs and so doubles as a table. Thick rope is tied to the tray at either end to make handles, in imitation of the thongs in the middle of Japanese shoes. The edges of the tray are finished with a thin veneer strip.

Tea-house Tray

Materials & Equipment

- Piece of 25mm (1in) MDF (medium-density fibreboard), 70 x 35cm (28 x 14in), for tray top
- Scrap wood • Pencil and ruler
- Clamp
- Protective face mask
- Hand drill with 25mm (1in) and 6mm (¼in) drill bits
- Hacksaw
- 42cm (16 in) wooden dowel, 25mm (1in) in diameter
- Fine-grade sandpaper
- Waterproof wood adhesive
- Water-based acrylic wood primer
- Paintbrush
- Pistachio-green oil-based satin-finish (eggshell) paint
- Fusible veneer strip • Brown paper
- Iron • Craft knife
- 120cm (48in) brown cord, 6mm (¼in) in diameter
- Masking tape

1 Place the tray top face down. Following the diagram at the back of the book, mark 10cm (4in) down and 6cm (2½in) in from the long edge at each corner, for the legs.

2 Clamp the tray top firmly and, wearing a face mask, use a 25mm (1in) drill bit to drill halfway through the MDF at each point.

3 Turn the tray top over. Mark two points 6cm (2½in) down and 10cm (4in) in from the long edge at each side. Re-clamp the MDF and drill a hole through each point using a 6mm (¼in) bit, to make holes for the rope handles.

4 Using a hacksaw, clamp and cut four pieces of dowel 10.5cm (4in) long to make the tray legs. Sand the ends smooth. Spread waterproof wood adhesive on the end of each leg and in each hole in the tray top. Press the legs firmly into the holes, removing any excess adhesive with a damp cloth. Leave to dry thoroughly.

5 Apply a coat of acrylic wood primer to the tray. When dry, add two coats of pistachio-green satin-finish (eggshell) paint and leave to dry.

6 Using scissors, cut four lengths of veneer strip slightly longer than the sides of the tray. Stand the tray on end. Position the first strip of veneer, lining it up with the top edge of the tray. Cover the veneer with a piece of brown paper and, following the manufacturer's instructions, bond it to the tray using an iron. Trim the end and repeat to attach the remaining strips.

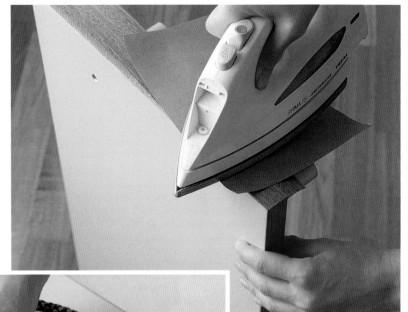

7 Using a craft knife, carefully trim away the excess veneer from the sides of the tray. Lightly smooth the cut edges with fine-grade sandpaper.

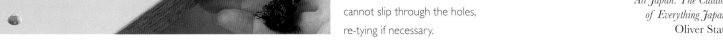

8 Cut two 60cm (24in) lengths of brown cord. Tie a large double knot at one end. Bind the remaining end with masking tape. Thread the cords through the holes at either side of the tray to make the handles. Remove the masking tape and knot the remaining ends to secure the handles. Make sure the handles cannot slip through the holes, re-tying if necessary.

> *" The tea ceremony cannot be learned from books. Like Zen Buddhism...it too can be transmitted only from master to disciple. "*
>
> All Japan: The Catalogue
> of Everything Japanese
> Oliver Statler

japan
The Conservatory

❝ *The Japanese garden is*

fundamentally based on nature and natural

forms, but interpreted in a manner

totally distinct from the western conception

of these terms. ❞

The Art of the Garden
Miles Hadfield

Zen Gardens

Perhaps the best-known Japanese gardens are the abstract rock-and-sand gardens built around Zen temples. These form arid, austerely beautiful, non-representational landscapes, with the carefully positioned rocks denoting islands and mountains in an expanse of sand. The sand may be raked into straight lines, ripples, curves and circles, suggesting water. The most celebrated example of this type of garden is found at the Ryoanji temple in Kyoto.

The table-top Zen garden is a small-scale aid to contemplation. The sides of a plain, square table are extended upwards to make a tray structure to hold sand. Two or three pleasingly shaped rocks are arranged in the slightly moist sand, which is raked into simple patterns with a wide-toothed comb.

Rock-garden Table

Materials & Equipment

- Wooden table • Protective face mask
- Medium-grade sandpaper and sanding block
- Waterproof wood adhesive
- 4 strips of 18mm (⅝in) MDF (medium-density fibreboard), each 12cm (4½in) wide x length of the table top plus 18mm (⅝in)
- 25mm (1in) panel pins (tacks) and hammer
- 4 strips of 10mm (⅜in) MDF, each 10cm (4in) wide x inside length of table top minus 10mm (⅜in)
- 20mm (¾in) panel pins (tacks)
- Fine-grade sandpaper
- Filler and filling knife
- Acrylic wood primer • Paintbrush
- Brown satin-finish (eggshell) oil-based paint
- Rocks • Sand • Wide-toothed comb
- Sheet of 4mm (⅛in) perspex (plexiglass), cut to fit table top and polished

1 Wearing a face mask and working outdoors if possible, sand the table. Lay the table on its side. Spread a line of waterproof wood adhesive along one side of the table top. Press a strip of 18mm (⅝in) MDF into the adhesive, lining up the lower edges and one side, so that the second side overlaps the opposite corner.

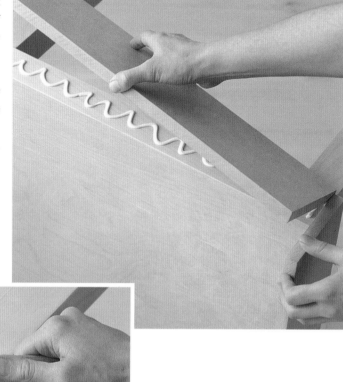

2 Tap in 25mm (1in) panel pins (tacks) to hold the MDF in place. Wipe off any excess adhesive using a damp cloth. Turn the table over again to expose the next edge, and attach the second piece of MDF in the same way, butting the sides together. Repeat to attach the remaining MDF.

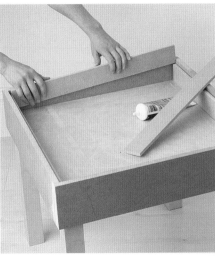

3 Spread wood adhesive on the backs of the 10mm (⅜in) MDF rebate (rabbet) strips. Glue them inside the outer wall of the table, butting the sides together as before. Hold them in place with 20mm (¾in) panel pins (tacks).

4 Wearing a face mask, lightly sand the corners of the table. Fill them if necessary and leave to dry. Prime the table, then apply two coats of mid-brown satin-finish (eggshell) wood paint.

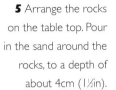

5 Arrange the rocks on the table top. Pour in the sand around the rocks, to a depth of about 4cm (1½in).

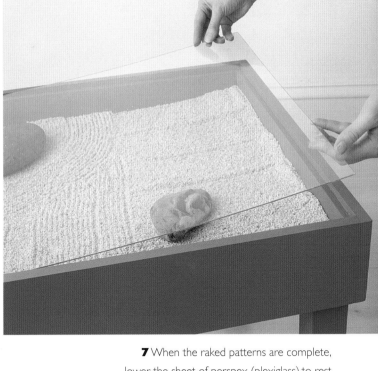

6 Using a wide-toothed comb, rake the sand into straight and curved lines. If you are not satisfied with the results, simply flatten the sand and start again.

7 When the raked patterns are complete, lower the sheet of perspex (plexiglass) to rest on the rebate (rabbet) in the top of the table. To change the rocks or the patterns in the sand, simply remove the perspex.

Raked Sand

The dry gardens known in Japan as *kansho-niwa*, and in the west as Zen gardens, were developed by Japanese Zen priests as an aid to contemplation and meditation. The basic design principles laid down around the twelfth century are still used today to create 'landscapes' of rocks in a 'sea' of pale sand. No other elements are used, and the sand is raked into lines and swirls to convey a feeling of moving water.

This cushion is made by stitching together two squares of fleece fabric to make a thick pad. The design is marked on the front of the fabric, then sewn using closely spaced lines of machine stitch, to give a quilted effect. The simple, graphic design, made up of circles and lines, is based on the raked sand patterns of Zen gardens.

Zen Cushion

Materials & Equipment

- 70cm (28in) grey fleece fabric, 140cm (56in) wide
- Scissors
- Dressmaker's pins
- Pair of compasses (compass)
- Thin card (cardboard)
- Soft pencil
- 70cm (28in) pale blue fleece fabric, 90cm (36in) wide
- Sewing machine and threads to match fabrics

1 For the cushion front, cut two 63cm (25in) squares of grey fleece fabric. Pin the squares together, one on top of the other, matching the edges and corners exactly.

2 Using a pair of compasses (compass), draw a circle 20cm (8in) in diameter onto thin card (cardboard) and cut it out to make a template. Referring to the diagram at the back of the book, place the template in the upper left-hand corner of the cushion front and draw around it with a soft pencil. Repeat in the upper right-hand corner to make a second circle.

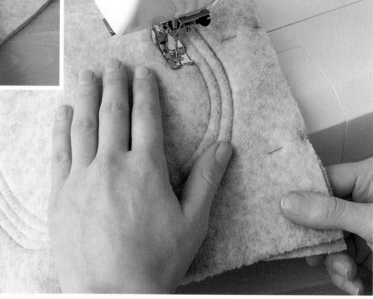

3 Machine stitch around the first circle using matching thread, following the pencil line. Use a long, straight stitch, otherwise the fabric will pucker. Complete the circle, place the machine foot against the stitching as a width gauge, and then continue sewing around to make a spiral pattern. Repeat for the second circle.

5 Starting 20cm (8in) in from the left-hand edge of the cushion, mark and stitch 15 equally spaced shorter lines at right angles to the quilted band. Position the template in the bottom right-hand corner of the cushion, with the upper half overlapping the fabric. Draw around the template onto the fabric and stitch concentric lines as before.

4 Mark nine equally spaced horizontal lines, starting 2cm (¾in) below the circles. Stitch along these to form a quilted band across the centre of the cushion.

6 To make the cushion back, cut two pieces of pale blue fleece fabric each measuring 63 × 40cm (25 × 16in). Turn under and pin a 1.5cm (½in) hem down one long edge of each piece of fleece and machine stitch using matching thread.

7 With right sides facing, pin one half of the cushion back to the cushion front. Pin the second half on top, overlapping at the centre to make a flap. Stitch the front to the back using a 1.5cm (½in) seam allowance.

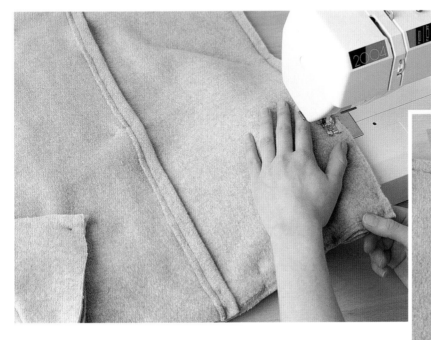

8 Clip the cushion corners diagonally, just above the seam. Trim the seams and turn through the cushion cover. If necessary, use a pin to pull out the corners to sharp points.

The Tea Ceremony

The Japanese tea ceremony is a ritualized performance, influenced by Zen Buddhism, where every action is carefully considered. The host of the ceremony enters the tea room and prepares green tea for each of the guests in turn. The style of tea bowls, caddies and other accessories varies according to the season and an appropriate flower and an artwork are placed in the *tokonoma*, a specially designed wall recess.

This painted tea set is decorated with simple, graphic designs inspired by Japanese calligraphy. They are drawn freehand, directly onto the china, giving a spontaneity to the overall design. To give the china a simple, almost monochrome appearance, only two colours of paint have been chosen.

Painted Tea Set

Materials & Equipment

- Plain Japanese-style tea set
- Vinegar
- Cotton wool
- Chinagraph (charcoal) pencil
- Cold-set, water-based ceramic paint in pewter-grey and yellow-ochre
- Thin, pointed artist's paintbrush
- Narrow, flat artist's paintbrush

1 Wash each piece of china in a solution of warm water and vinegar to remove any grease from the surface. Dry thoroughly using a clean tea towel.

2 Draw a simple freehand design onto each item using a chinagraph (charcoal) pencil. The designs can cover one or both sides.

4 Using yellow-ochre paint, fill in the circular areas of the designs and leave to dry. Use a slightly wider, flatter paintbrush to apply the paint.

3 Paint the pewter-grey patterns onto the china using a thin, pointed paintbrush. Add a little water to the paint if it is too thick. If you make a mistake, simply wipe off the paint before it dries and start again.

5 Using the wider paintbrush, add the broad sweeps of yellow-ochre paint to the teapot and the sugar bowl. Leave to dry.

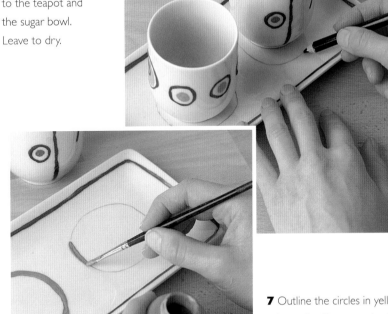

6 Paint a thin, pewter-grey border around the edge of the tray. When the paint is dry, position the cups on the tray and draw loosely around them with the chinagraph (charcoal) pencil.

7 Outline the circles in yellow-ochre paint. Decorate the lids of the teapot and sugar bowl. Leave all the china to dry for 72 hours before using it.

Templates

All templates shown actual size unless otherwise stated.

←8CM (3IN)→ PIECE OF GARDEN TRELLIS, 3 SQUARES × 3 SQUARES ←8CM (3IN)→

USE 15MM (½IN) BIRCH-FACED PLY, CUT TO LENGTH OF TRELLIS

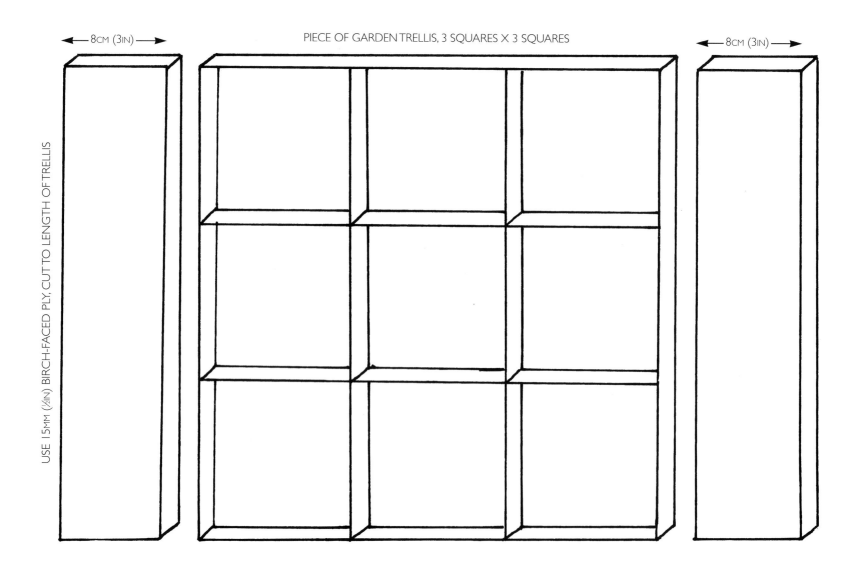

Wall Light   p36

Geisha Bag   p40

Reduce to 55%

BAG AND LINING BASE (CUT 1)

BAG AND LINING GUSSET (CUT 2)

BAG ONLY HANDLE (CUT 2)

Geisha Bag   p40

Enlarge by 200%

BAG AND LINING FRONT AND BACK (CUT 2)

Geisha Bag   p40

Enlarge by 200%

USE 18MM (⅝IN) THICK MDF

SIDE WALL (CUT 2)

AT EACH END, DRILL 2CM (¾IN) IN FROM BOTH
EDGES TO SCREW SIDES TOGETHER

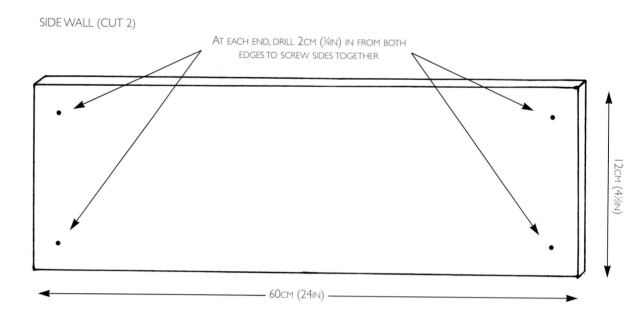

12CM (4¾IN)

60CM (24IN)

END WALL (CUT 2)

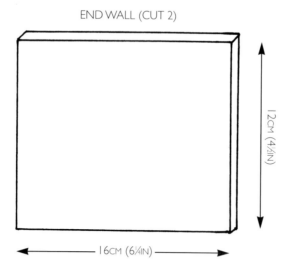

12CM (4¾IN)

16CM (6¼IN)

Plaster Candleholder   p54

BASE (CUT 1)

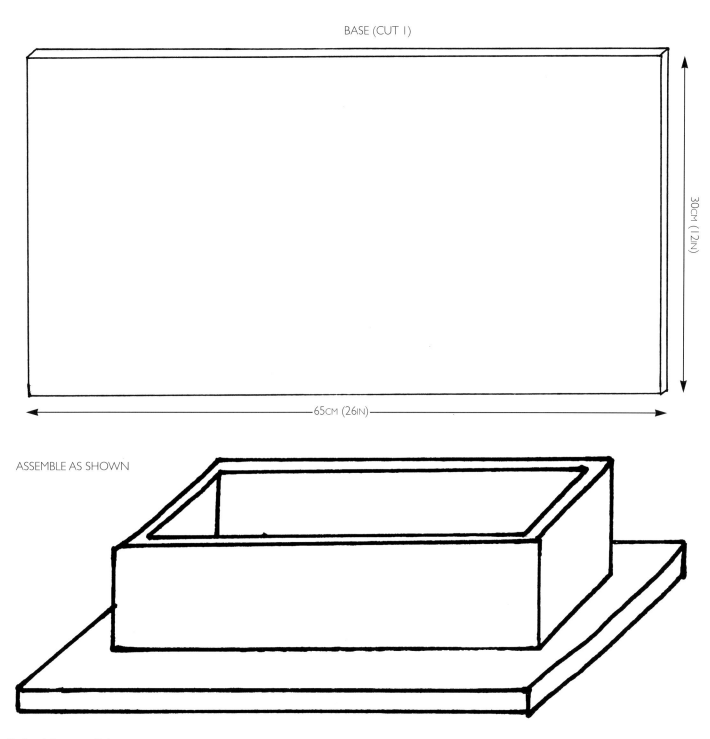

30CM (12IN)

65CM (26IN)

ASSEMBLE AS SHOWN

Plaster Candleholder   p54

Flower Border p60

FRONT

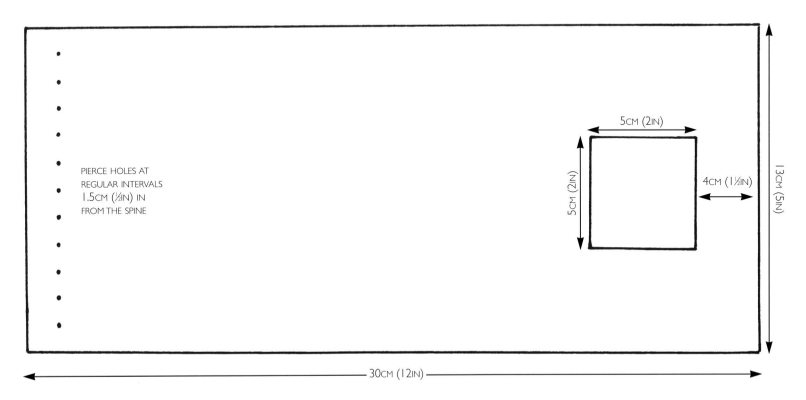

PIERCE HOLES AT
REGULAR INTERVALS
1.5CM (½IN) IN
FROM THE SPINE

5CM (2IN)

5CM (2IN)

4CM (1½IN)

13CM (5IN)

30CM (12IN)

Hand-bound Books p64

USE 25MM (1IN) THICK MDF

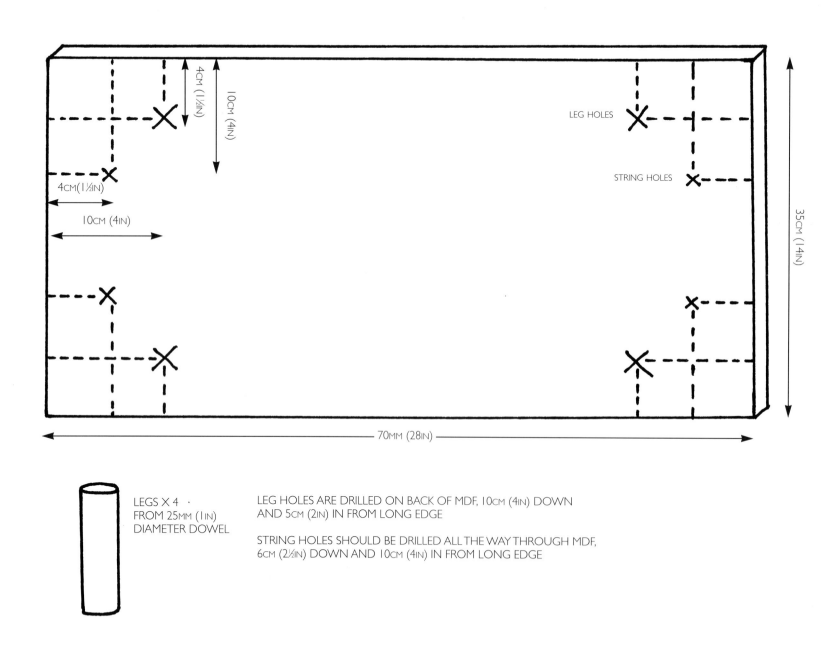

4CM (1½IN)

10CM (4IN)

4CM(1½IN)

10CM (4IN)

LEG HOLES

STRING HOLES

35CM (14IN)

70MM (28IN)

LEGS × 4 ·
FROM 25MM (1IN)
DIAMETER DOWEL

LEG HOLES ARE DRILLED ON BACK OF MDF, 10CM (4IN) DOWN
AND 5CM (2IN) IN FROM LONG EDGE

STRING HOLES SHOULD BE DRILLED ALL THE WAY THROUGH MDF,
6CM (2½IN) DOWN AND 10CM (4IN) IN FROM LONG EDGE

Tea-house Tray   p68

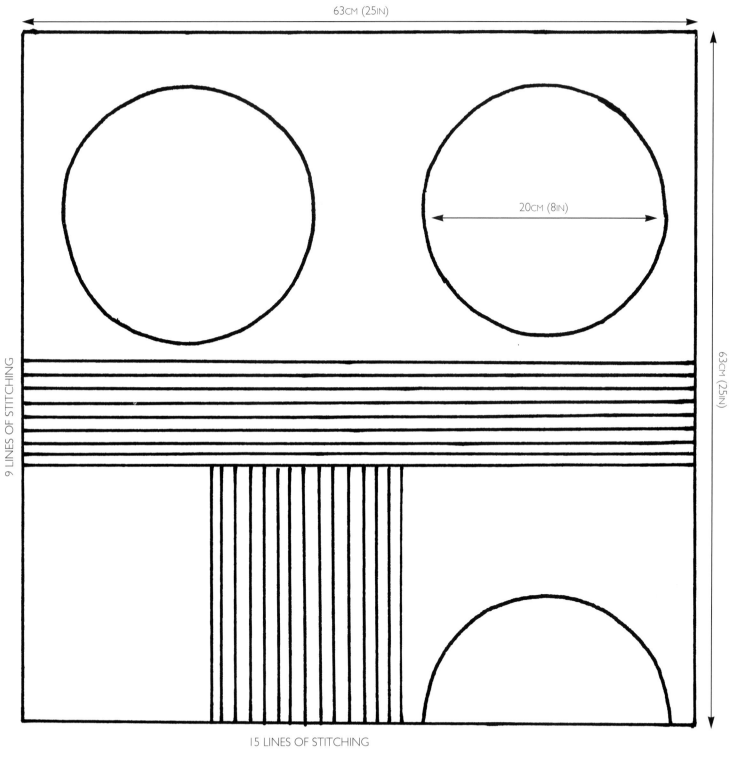

63CM (25IN)

20CM (8IN)

63CM (25IN)

9 LINES OF STITCHING

15 LINES OF STITCHING

Zen Cushion p78

Further Information

Cultural Organizations

Japan-America Society of Washington, DC
1020 19th Street, NW LL40
Washington, DC 20036
Tel: (202) 883-2210
Fax: (202) 833-2456
website: www.us-japan.org/dc

Japan Centre Bookshop
212 Piccadilly
London W1
Tel: 020 7439 8035

Japan National Tourist Organization
Heathcote House
20 Savile Row
London W1
Tel: 020 7734 9638

Japan Society
333 East 47th Street
New York, NY 10017
Tel: (212) 832-1155
Fax: (212) 755-6752
website: www.jpnsoc.com

UK Suppliers

The Cane Store
Blackstock Road
London N4
Tel: 020 7354 4210
Bamboo

TN Lawrence
119 Clerkenwell Road
London EC1
Tel: 020 7242 3534
Handmade Japanese paper

McCulloch and Wallis Ltd
25 Dering Street
London W1
Tel: 020 7629 0311
Trimmings

VV Rouleaux Ltd
6 Marylebone High Street
London W1
Tel: 020 7224 5179
Trimmings

Alec Tiranti
27 Warren Street
London W1
Tel: 020 7636 8565
Casting plaster and sculpture supplies

US Suppliers

Frank's Cane and Rush Supply
7252 Heil Avenue
Huntington Beach, CA 92647
Tel: (714) 847-0707
Fax: (714) 843-5645
website: www.franksupply.com
Bamboo

Ichiyo Art Centre, Inc.
432 East Paces Ferry Road
Atlanta, GA 30305
Tel: (404) 233-1846
Fax: (404) 233-8012
website: *www.ichiyoart.com*
Paper and other Japanese craft supplies

Nichi Bei Bussan
140 East Jackson Street
San Jose, CA 95112
Tel: (408) 294-8048
Fax: (408) 294-2158
website: www.nbstore.com
Japanese fabrics and other Japanese products

Sculpture House Casting
155 West 26th Street
New York, NY 10001
Tel: (888) 374-8665
Fax: (212) 645-3717
website: www.sculptshop.com
Casting plaster and other sculpture supplies

Index

Acknowledgements

Author's Acknowledgements

I would like to thank all the people who made producing this book such a pleasure:
Neil Hadfield, as ever, for his support and enthusiasm, and for making the Tea-house Tray, Wall Lights, Bamboo Duckboard, Display Board and Plaster Candleholder with such skill; Lynda Watts for the impeccably sewn Patchwork Quilt; Ali Myer and Cheryl Brown for their vision and enthusiasm, especially at the start of the project; Stewart Grant for his great photography and, with Ginette Chapman, generous hospitality; Mia Pejcinovic for her style; Kevan for set-building; Amanda and Carmen for cheerfully working late; Valerie Streak for picture research; Sarah Widdicombe for her sharp eyes and Lindsay Porter, who, with Ali Myer, pulled it all together with such style.

Publishers' Acknowledgements

The publishers would also like to thank the following for lending items for photography:

The Kitchen
Jussi table, Roy stool: Ikea (020 8208 5607); white ceramic bowls: Bouchon (020 8740 9744); fake orchids, flip flops, Chinese flask, shopping bag: Kitschen Sync (020 7497 5129); scented candles, beakers: Monsoon Home (020 7313 3000)

The Bedroom
Teak bedside tables, leather storage boxes: The Holding Company (020 7352 1600); futon bed: Ikea (020 8208 5607); Triomphe Sand bedlinen: Yves Delorme (0113 243 4448); mulberry Mongolian lambswool rugs: Stepan Tertsakian (020 7236 8788)

The Bathroom
Bamboo ladder: The Holding Company (020 7352 1600); selection of candles from the Chinese Herbal Therapy range: Prices (020 7228 3345); Zen bucket, ladle, bamboo planter, bamboo soap dish: Emily Readett-Bayley (020 7231 3939); Japanese slippers: Neal Street East (020 7240 0135); bamboo jug: Monsoon Home (020 7313 3000)

The Study
Suede floor cushion: Ocean (0870 848 4840); willow: Elephant (020 7637 7930); close up: Singapore table: The Pier (020 7814 5004)

The Conservatory
Singapore armchair: The Pier (020 7814 5004); suede cube, terracotta tea-light holder: Ocean (0870 848 4840); bamboo screen: The Holding Company (020 7352 1600); incense coil: Bouchon (020 8740 9744); oblique cut bamboo vases: Emily Readett-Bayley (020 7231 3939)

Picture Credits

All photographs are by Stewart Grant, except the following: Aspect Picture Library/Bob Davis pages 62–3; CORBIS/Bruce Burkhardt pages 30–1; CORBIS/Owen Franken pages 24–5; CORBIS/Michael S. Yamashita pages 48–9; The Garden Picture Library/Mark Bolton pages 44–5; HAGA/Britstock – IFA pages 16-17, 52-3, 58-9, 80-1; Japan National Tourist Organization pages 20–1, 66-7, 72–3; Telegraph Colour Library pages 34–5, 38–9, 74–5

Front cover, below, Aspect Picture Library/Bob Davis

Bibliography

An Illustrated Encyclopaedia of Traditional Symbols, J C Cooper, Thames and Hudson, 1990

The Art of the Garden, Miles Hadfield, Studio Vista, 1965

Papermaking: The History and Technique of an Ancient Craft, Dard Hunter, Dover Books, 1978

The Pillow Book of Sei Shonagon, translated and edited by Ivan Morris, Penguin Books, 1971

Culture Shock! Japan, Rex Shelley, Kuperard, 1993

Japanese Style, Slesin, Cliff, Rozensztroch and De Chabaneix, Thames and Hudson, 1987

All Japan: The Catalogue of Everything Japanese, various authors with introduction by Oliver Statler, Quarto Books, 1984

For further information about the author, visit her website at www.marionelliot.co.uk